Newton Abbot
DEVON

Hi there,

My name is Toby, and I am a Dalmatian.

My walker (human) takes me on loads of lovely walks that are just perfect for dogs. My doggy friends and I were wondering if all our canine buddies knew about these walks. So, I decided to sit down and write a guide.
As I love to play, I will try and let you know if you are likely to meet any other dogs to play with or to sniff.
I will try and let you know about all the good things and any not so good features of any walk.
I will also let you know if there are any poo bins for your walker, as they don't seem to like poo as much as we do.
If you know of any walks that I don't know about, let me know so I can check them out and possibly include them in the next book. If you send me a picture of yourself I'll put it with your walk.

Enjoy your new walks,

Toby
Email me: toby@scrivenhousebooks.co.uk

Walk 1 - Teign Valley

Grid Reference: 859 735– Landranger 191 Distance: 1.5 miles (1 hour)

I love this walk. It is the best place if you want to find other dogs to play with. The walkers will love it because they can park their cars in a car park and they have a nice river to look at. There are sometimes a few cows at the far end of the walk but not very often and they are easily avoided. There is loads of water to play in and lots of space to run in. If you want sticks to chase you'd better do the walk in reverse and visit the woods first. My brother Domino comes sometimes and is in one photo.

1. First get your walker to park in the car park. Be careful in the car park because the road running past is very busy. Let your walker put a lead on you just to be sure.
2. Cross the main road and through the gate. Please shut the gate as a few of my friends have got excited in the past and have dashed through across the road on the way back to their owner's car.
3. Now simply follow the river bank along for about a mile. You will pass lots of places where you can leap into the river and have a swim or paddle. Be careful on one section as the river bank is quite obviously crumbling. You and your walkers will have to keep an eye out for cows, as they are very occasionally around grazing. They are used to people, so as long as your walkers put you on your lead until you get around the next bend, all will be fine.
4. After about a mile, you will find a bridge on your right. Cross the bridge, turn right, and then walk back down the other side of the river.
5. You will reach a fork in the path where you can either turn right and walk along the river bank (some tricky bits), or take the easier path on your left that also takes you back.
6. When you get near the road, both paths lead you left a bit before letting you out onto the road itself.
7. Once on the road turn right and walk back to the car park. Watch out, it can be busy here.

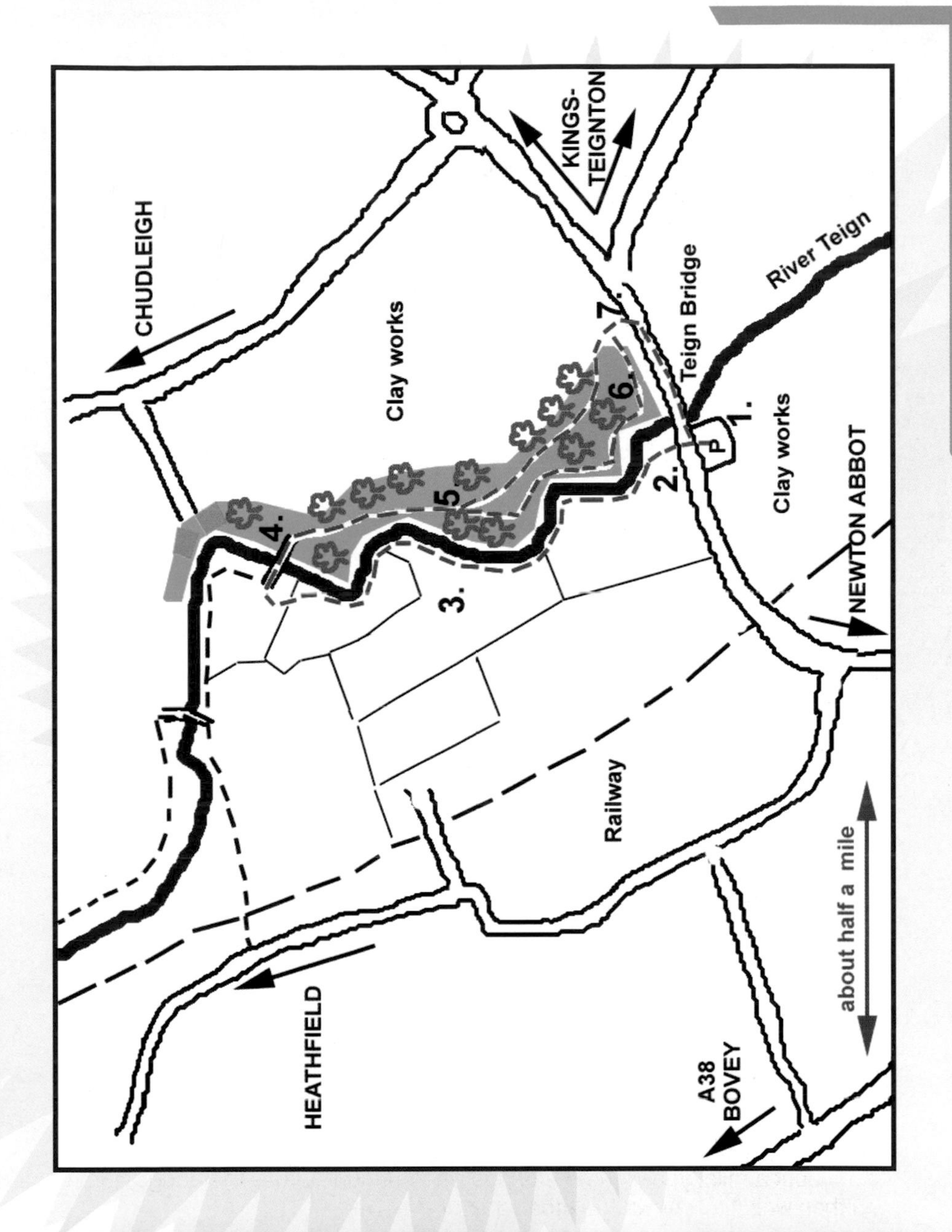

Playmates?	Y	Water to play in?	Y	Running space?	Y
Are there any hills?	N	Any tricky stiles?	N	Car Parking?	Y
Are farm animals likely?	Y	Poo Bins?	Y	Plenty of sticks?	Y

Walk 2 - Bovey River at Parke

Grid Reference: 811 784—Landranger 191 Distance: 2miles (1.5 hours)

This is another lovely walk with lots of other dogs to get involved with. The scenery on this walk is fantastic and I love to stop in the dappled shade by the river and have a paddle. There are a few stiles and gates, but they are all very dog friendly. My owner sometimes gets frustrated by the parking but it seems passable to me. I often hear my owners say that part of the walk is an old railway line (whatever that is). I really recommend this walk. My brother Domino loves this walk when he stays over.

1. Once you get past the Bovey Roundabout pull over onto the gravel area to your left. You will probably see other cars parked there. Then walk down the side of the road to find the gate into Parke. Make sure that your owners put you on a lead as the road is fast.
2. Once in the gate, turn right and walk until you get to the lovely bridge over the river (some humans play poo sticks here, what a funny thing to do with poo!)
3. After the bridge turn left down some steps to the river bank. Then walk on with the river on your left. This is a great field for running in!
4. Follow the river until you get to a stile with a special dog section. Over the stile and turn left, following the river. You will go round a narrow path here above the river so tread carefully.
5. Then down the steps, across a small footbridge and out into the next clearing past the big tree bench and straight through to the opposite end.
6. Once you are back in the woods, go about 20 feet and then turn left across a little wooden gangway to the river bank and then follow the river again
7. You will pass another field on your right which is good for running in
8. Just round the next corner you will find a lovely weir and then a beach with a great bench for your walkers to sit on whilst you take a paddle.
9. Further up, the path bends away from the river up into the woods. Follow the path up into the woods where you will join the old railway line that is raised up on an embankment. Turn right down this path and follow it all the way back to the car parking area.

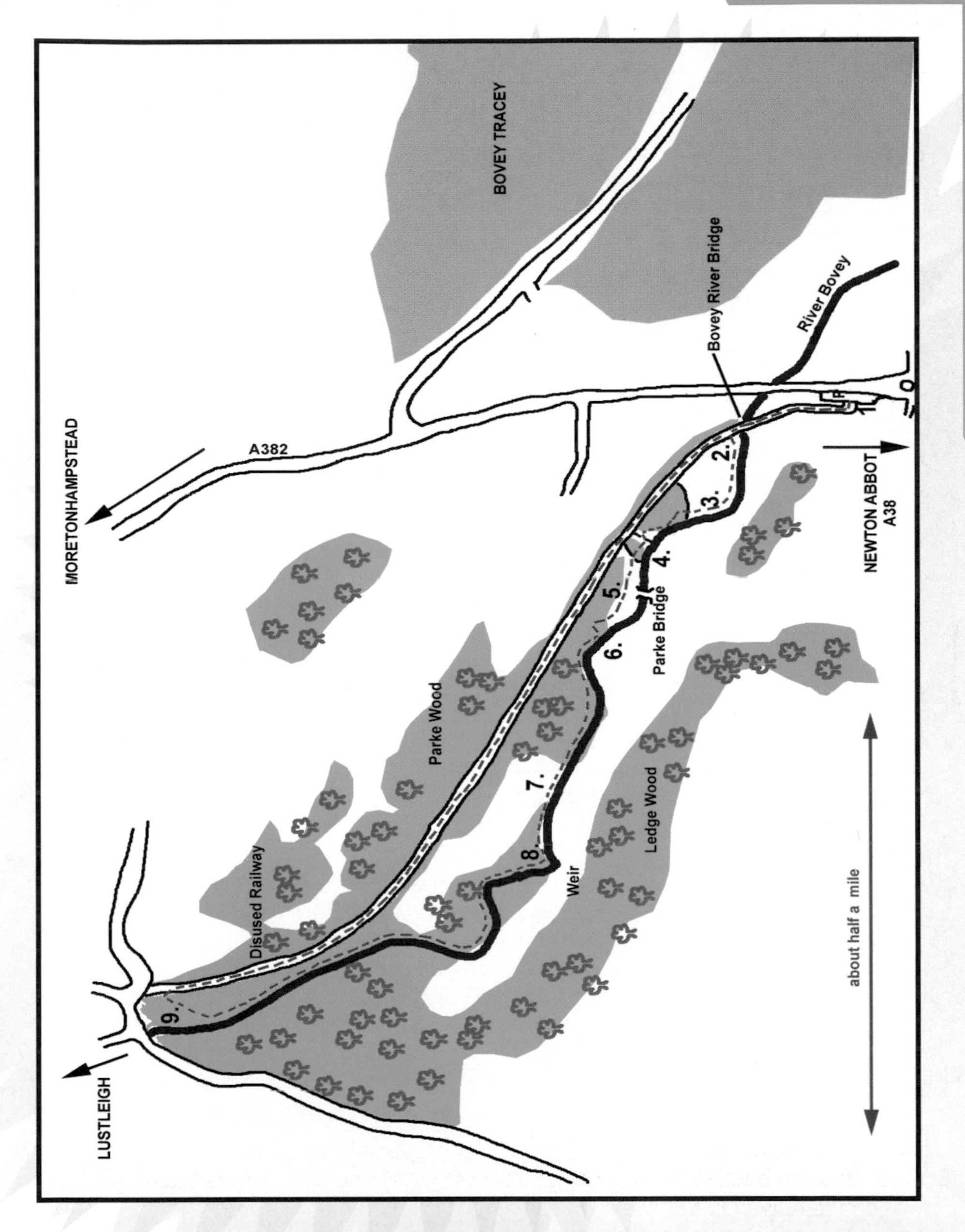

Playmates?	Y	Water to play in?	Y	Running space?	Y
Are there any hills?	N	Any tricky stiles?	N	Car Parking?	Y
Are farm animals likely?	N	Poo Bins?	Y	Plenty of sticks?	Y

Walk 3 - Bovey Plantation

Grid Reference: 823 748—Landranger 191 Distance: 1.5miles (1hour)

This is an interesting walk. There are sometimes other dogs to play with, but I like this walk because of the lovely woods and heath, which is beautiful in the autumn. This walk is great because you are really just following a short part of the Templar Way, so there are quite a few signs to help.

1. Follow the Liverton and Blackpool signs at the Drum Bridges roundabout.
2. Drive about half a mile up this road with the woods on your right.
3. Pull into the first road on your left and park up opposite Old Liverton Road. There is an entrance to the plantation just opposite the road your walker has parked in.
4. Enter the plantation (turn around and look behind you at this point as you will have to recognise the yellow bungalow at the end of your walk to find your way back) now follow the track for about half a mile, you will go straight on at two smaller cross roads, until you get to an obvious cross roads of the two main paths in the plantation. The paths are very wide at this point, big enough for a car.
5. Go straight on here, down a dip, until you reach another cross roads. Turn left. Follow this path which will start to narrow. The path will bare left keep following path you are on.
6. Another big gravel path will join yours from the right, ignore this and carry straight on, now follow track markers for the Templar way. Go straight on at next T-junction. Carry on into the woods following Templar Way signs. I always stop for a quick play and a drink at the little bridge in the woods.
7. Your path will then be crossed by one of the main paths, carry straight on over following a narrow track across the heath this is still the Templar Way.
8. At next cross roads go straight on into the woods and then turn left after a little footbridge. At the next cross roads follow the sign right. Then go left after another little bridge and follow path through woods. You are still on the Templar Way.
9. Now you have to keep your eyes peeled for the yellow bungalow. You will come to a slightly bigger junction which is the path you started on. You need to turn right here to get back to the car and the yellow bungalow (unless they paint it another colour!)

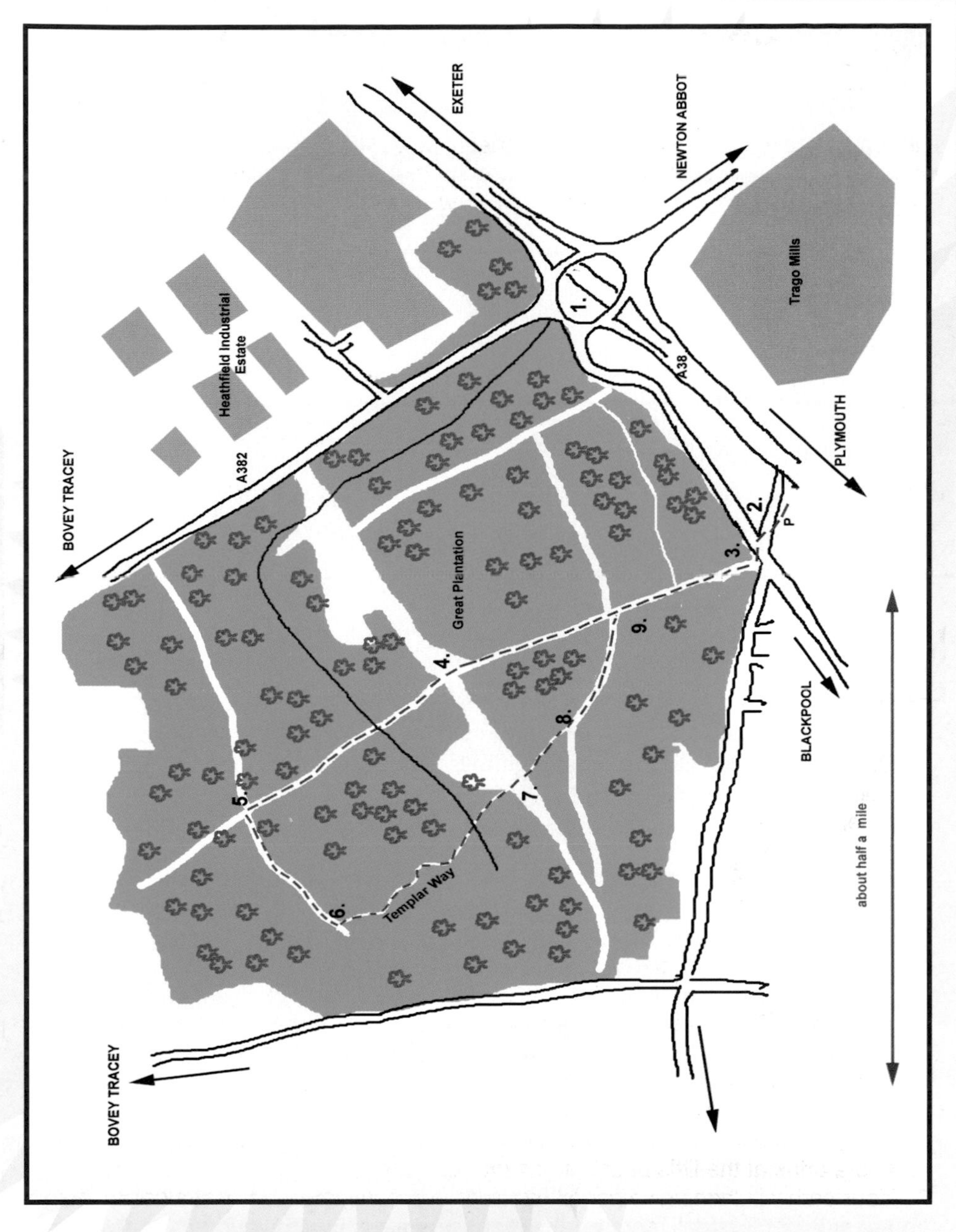

Playmates?	Y	Water to play in?	Y	Running space?	Y
Are there any hills?	N	Any tricky stiles?	N	Car Parking?	Y
Are farm animals likely?	N	Poo Bins?	Y	Plenty of sticks?	Y

Walk 4 - Haldon Hills

Grid Reference: 884 847 – Landranger 192 Distance: 2.5miles (1.5hours)

Haldon hills has many tracks some with great views. I know that my walkers like nice views so I have tried to choose the best walk that has a bit of everything. Once you get to know Haldon Hills you may try your own routes.

1. Either turn off the A38 or A380 following signs for Dunchideock and Forest Park, drive along the road along the top of the ridge past a crossroads with signs to Chudleigh (left) and Exeter (right), then about another 500 yards on your left you take a turning into the Haldon Hills Forest Park.
2. Drive in and find a good place to park. There is a poo bin near the car park entrance. Parking costs a pound, but there are good facilities here.
3. Now follow the 'Play Trail' yellow marker posts out of the car park until you reach the first set of play ropes and swings. Walk past these, keeping them on your right, and head toward an old notice board at the bottom of the clearing. You then go down the steep track next to the noticeboard.
4. Halfway down the steep slope you will see a footpath on your left. Follow this footpath. You will eventually appear at a very large crossroads with lots of tracks leading off.
5. Carry straight on across the junction taking the Family Cycle trail up a hill on the left. Follow this as it wiggles gently up the hill. As you get to the top it does a sharp left, at this point take the footpath that leads off to the right.
6. Stay with the path until it leads you down into a tunnel of small trees. You will pass two kissing gates, then a small piece of fence crossing the path. You will then reach a wider boggy section with a very large tree (I love to get muddy paws here). On the other side of this small marshy bit you will find a turning on your right, with a small post with a metal plaque on top. Follow it down through some laurel trees and past a small lake on your left.
7. The path then opens up into a very wide gravel track which you follow for quite a way. This is a great place for some running around. There are also great views of the moor.
8. Finally you arrive at a T-junction where you turn right, back up the hill.
9. Follow this path back up all the way until you see the car parks on your left.

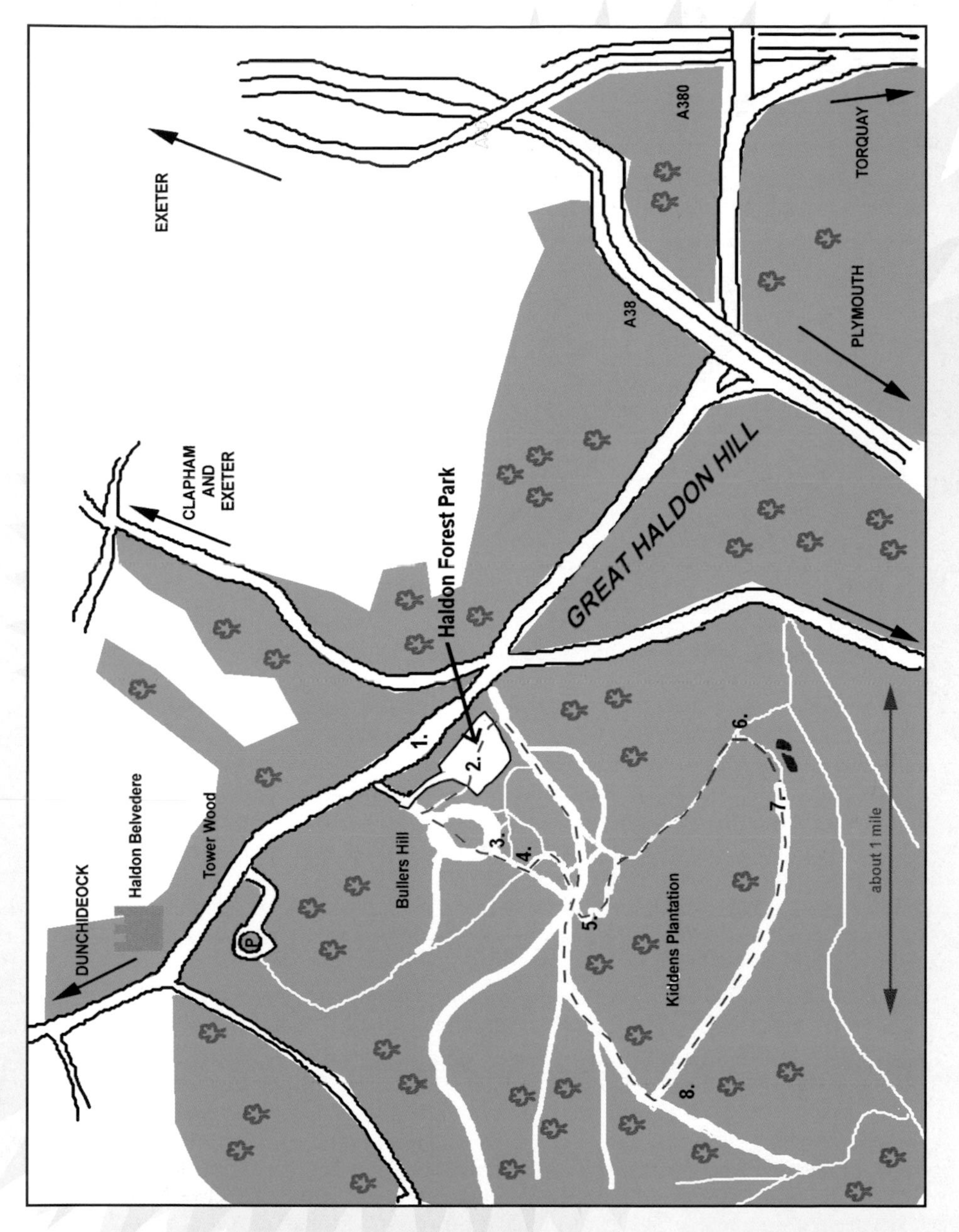

Playmates?	Y	Water to play in?	N	Running space?	Y
Are there any hills?	Y	Any tricky stiles?	N	Car Parking?	Y
Are farm animals likely?	N	Poo Bins?	Y	Plenty of sticks?	Y

Walk 5 - Under Castle Drogo

Grid Reference: 713 893—Landranger 191 Distance: 5 miles (3 hours)

If you and your walkers like views then this is a great walk. A few long climbs that are not particularly steep, and a long downhill that is moderately steep in places. There is even a pub to keep those walkers happy.

1. Follow signs to Moretonhampstead and then drive through the town following the A382 towards Drewsteignton. You will pass the Mill Hotel on your left. Just after this you will cross Dogmarsh Bridge. After the bridge pull over in the lay by on the left. Then cross the road and through the gate on the opposite side.
2. Follow the riverbank downstream through the two fields. If there are cows out, you can cross the first footbridge to the other side of the river and walk down the right bank until you reach the next footbridge.
3. Whichever side of the river Teign you are on, you must be back on the left hand side at the second footbridge. Here you leave the river and follow the Hunter's Path up the hill.
4. The path joins a quiet lane where my walkers tend to leave me off the lead. Follow this up the hill for about 300 yards. Then take the Hunter's Path through the gate on the right.
5. Now just follow the Hunter's path signs and enjoy the spectacular views. My walkers often take a rest on the amazing granite outcrops that jut into the valley.
6. Eventually the path drops down to the road. This one is a little more busy due to the pub. I normally stop and let my walkers put my lead on.
   Once you are on the road turn right and head for the pub.

7 & 8. When your walkers are stuffed full of grub you can set off home. You can walk back along either river bank, however I prefer to stay on the side the pub is on, it's simply prettier. If you're not good with steep slopes you may be better walking back on the other side. I love this bit of the walk because I get to play in the river all the way back. Lots of stick chasing to be had!
Just follow either path back to the weirs, with their fish ladder, and then cross the foot-bridge if you want to and then continue up the river back to the car

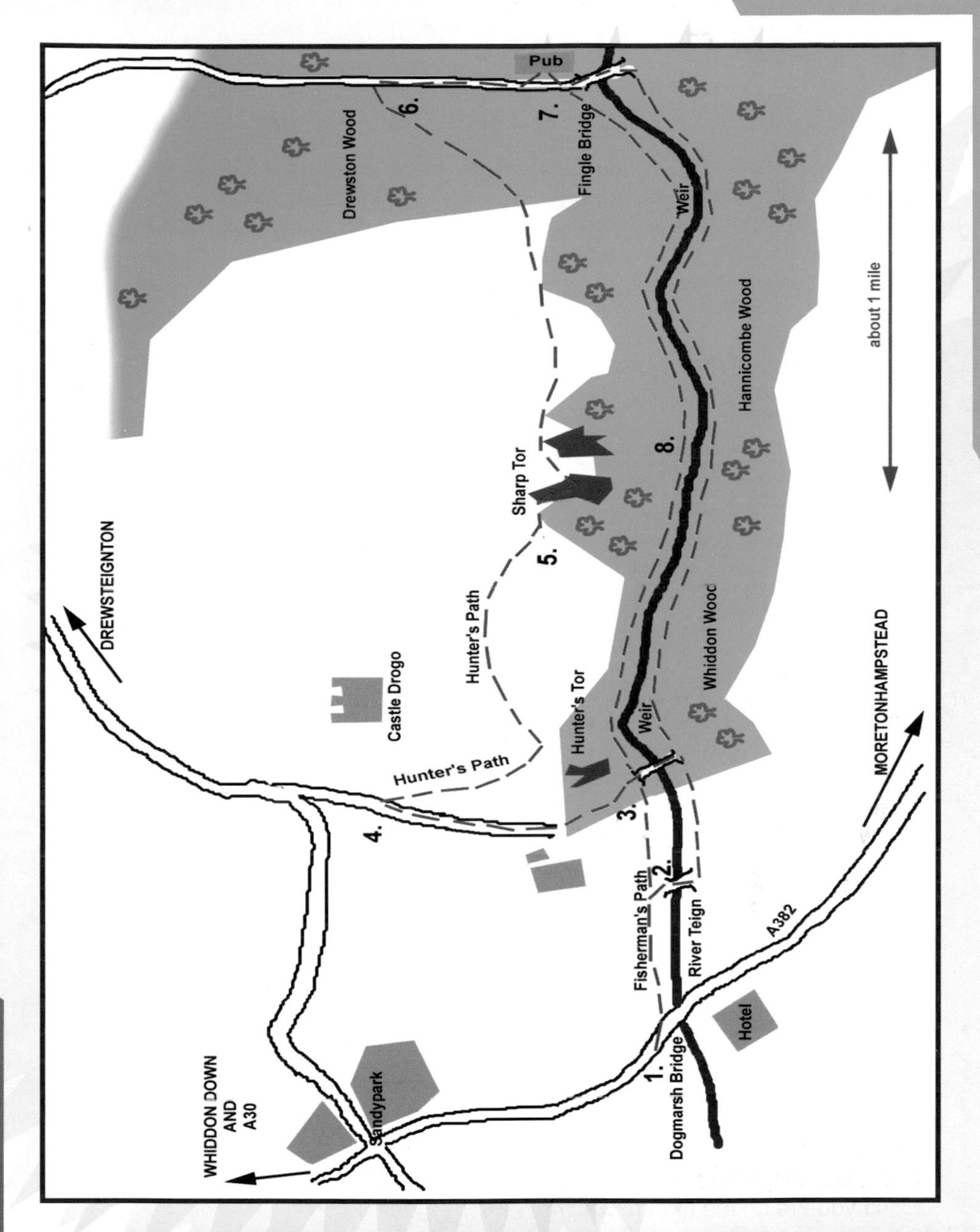

Playmates?	Y	Water to play in?	Y	Running space?	Y
Are there any hills?	Y	Any tricky stiles?	N	Car Parking?	Y
Are farm animals likely?	N	Poo Bins?	N	Plenty of sticks?	Y

Walk 6 - Upper Teign Reservoirs

Grid Reference: 803 823—Landranger 191 Distance: 5 miles (3 hours)

This is a great walk involving loads of lovely water, some woodlands and some really interesting things for your walkers to look at. There is a great view from the lanes half way around the walk, and there are lots of lovely smells for your nose. Please note that neither dogs or people should enter the reservoir water.

1. Having turned off the A382 Moretonhampstead road at Slade Cross (about 1km after a sharp downhill bend in the road) turn left at the top, drive until you see the car park on the right.
2. Once you are in the car park you need to leave via the path at the top end. Follow the path until you reach the edge of the lakes.
3. Then follow the path around the edge of the lakes. You need to cross over the first road and carry on around the edge of the next lake. When you reach the dam at the top of the second lake you need to cross the marsh at the end of the lake on the walkway. In spring keep an eye out for all the tadpoles! I always get very muddy trying to catch them (this would be a good time to get your walker to put your lead on).
4. Turn left once you have crossed the top of the lake, you will come up onto a road that crosses the bottom of Kennick Reservoir.
5. Turn left on this road and follow it for about half a mile.
6. Eventually you will find a lane leading off the road on your right. Follow this lane.
7. You will drop down to a stream that feeds the reservoir and you will then turn right onto a bridleway that leads back along the opposite side of Kennick Reservoir.
8. After a few yards you need to take the left fork, unless you want to disturb the fisherman along the bank of the lake.
9. Follow this bridle path through the woods. Ignoring signs at the first crossroads.
10. Eventually you reach a small brook and the bridleway turns into a lane running up a hill to your left. Follow this lane.
11. You will go past an old deserted farm/chapel owned by the Quaker's. Ignore a lane to your left, carry straight on. At the end of the lane you will meet a road.
12. Turn right on the road and walk down about 500 yards until you find a footpath on your left.

13. Take this footpath back to the banks of the Tottiford reservoir, and then follow the banks of the reservoir until you come out on a lane.
14. Walk straight on down the lane and across the dam at the bottom of all the reservoirs. Then take a right at the end of the dam onto a short footpath up the hill to the car park.

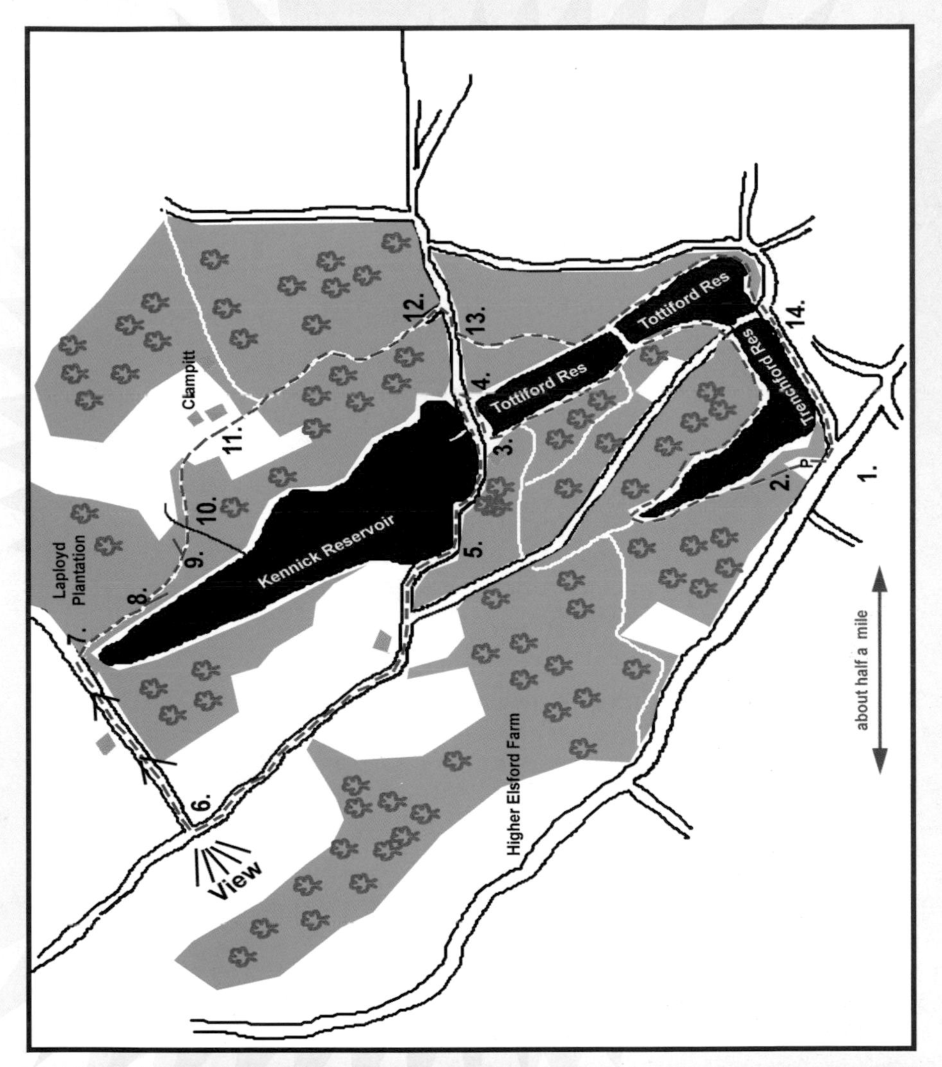

Playmates?	Y	Water to play in?	N	Running space?	Y
Are there any hills?	N	Any tricky stiles?	N	Car Parking?	Y
Are farm animals likely?	N	Poo Bins?	N	Plenty of sticks?	Y

Walk 7 - Kerswell Downs

Grid Reference: 874 677—Landranger 202 Distance: 1 mile (45mins)

Kerswell Downs is a lovely wooded walk, popular with any of my doggy friends who like chasing sticks and there are some lovely views on the way round for your walker. You will also hear lots of other dogs at Foredown Kennels having a short break from their walkers.

1. First get your walker to park in the car park on Foredown Hill, at the Kingskerswell end of Maddacombe Road.
2. Then take the path through the gate and up into the woods. There is a handrail here because this slope can get quite slippery for your walkers in the winter. Follow the handrail up onto the first common.
3. Cross the common and take the path directly opposite between the two hedges. You will hear Foredown Kennels from here.
4. Then straight across the next clearing and into the woods.
5. Now just stick to the path. You will pass a bench with a lovely view, where your walker may want to sit for a while. Then take the path on through the gap in the wall, ignoring the path to your left. (Update : The gap has been blocked and a new gateway made about 10 metres left along the wall. Go through the gateway and turn right back onto the path)
6. Follow the path through the woods and pass straight through the next clearing, ignoring a path to the left just afterwards. You will then get to the bottom end of a field, follow the path through the woods at the end of the field and up onto the common. Remember to pick a stick up here if you want your walker to throw it for you on the common.
7. Have a great play on the common. Then leave by the same entrance you came in, and walk back past the bottom of the field.
8. You will then come to a fork in the path, turn right.
9. You then just have to follow this path that will lead you under an interesting tree, and back through the wall in a different place.
10. You will then come to a clearing with three exits, take the path on the left. This will lead you back to the bench with the lovely view. Turn right and follow the path back to the car park.

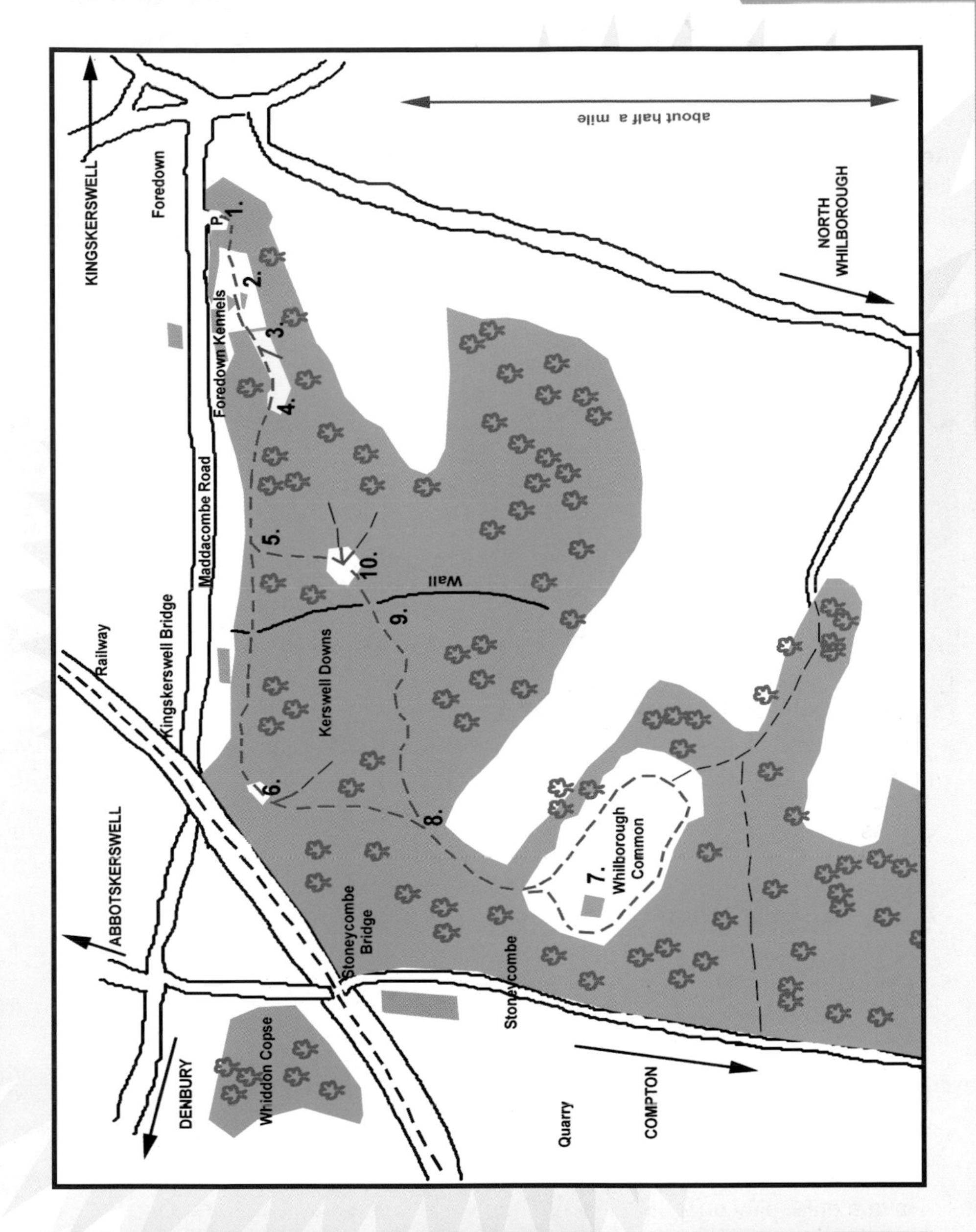

Playmates?	Y	Water to play in?	N	Running space?	Y
Are there any hills?	Y	Any tricky stiles?	N	Car Parking?	Y
Are farm animals likely?	N	Poo Bins?	Y	Plenty of sticks?	Y

Walk 8—Cockington Woods

Grid Reference: 895634—Landranger 202 Distance: 1 mile (1 hour)

This is a lovely walk in the heart of Torbay. It's another walk where you feel you could be miles from the town. Really beautiful countryside and lots of other routes to explore. Keep an eye out for my brother Domino because he lives nearby and loves this walk.

1. The easiest way to find the parking is to drive down Preston Down Road from Marldon. As you reach the steep part of the hill you will need to look for a turn on your left into Hilton Drive. Then take a left onto Cockington Lane, follow this, it will turn into Old Paignton Road. Then at the end of this road turn left and then right into Broadley Drive. Drive along Broadley Drive until the road turns sharp left. The path to the woods should be straight in front of you. Park up and enter the woods.
2. The path goes down steeply into the woods, follow the path down the hill ignoring paths to the left and right.
3. When you get to the Gatekeeper's Cottage take a sharp left following signs for Scadson woods. My Walkers often read the info about the local history.
4. You will then walk up a lovely path on the edges of the woods with a field and stream on your right, where you can stop and have a nice drink. At the end of the path you will reach Warren Barn. Take the path to the left of the barn that is again signposted to Scadson Woods.
5. At the next 4 way junction you follow the sign to Scadson Woods. Have a look around the woods and then take the path back to this junction and follow signs to Broadley Drive.
6. You will be walking through a new plantation of trees, I love to play hide and seek with my brother Domino when we walk here together .
7. When you get to the end of the plantation you will find a wooden gate. Don't go through the gate because it's nicer to turn left and walk down the side of the plantation and the woods. Follow this path down the hill at take a right at the bottom. Follow this path and it will bring you back to the start of the walk.

Playmates?	Y	Water to play in?	Y	Running space?	Y
Are there any hills?	Y	Any tricky stiles?	N	Car Parking?	Y
Are farm animals likely?	N	Poo Bins?	Y	Plenty of sticks?	Y

Walk 9 - The Dart at Kingswear

Grid Reference: 888 515—Landranger 202 Distance: 2.5 miles (1.5 hours)

This is one of my walker's favourite walks because of the stunning views of the River Dart and Dartmouth.

1. Head for Kingswear. You need to take the road marked `Lower Ferry' to Kingswear. You need to go around the one way system that takes you into the town. Then follow signs for Paignton back out of the town. You will dip down past the Marina car park and head back up the valley. Then you will need to find somewhere to park on your left. There are parking spaces opposite a new development. If you are stuck you may need to go round the one way system again and park just up the hill.
2. Walk up the hill away from the river. Until you find a gate on your left, with a public footpath sign above it. The sign on the gate is from the days of `Mad Cow' disease, ignore it.
3. Follow the path along through the woods and then drop down steeply to join a sleepy lane.
4. Turn right along the lane for about 100 metres.
5. Now enter Hoodown Wood and follow the path through the beautiful woods. You will eventually come out the other end onto an unadopted road. Follow this along enjoying the views of Dartmouth on your left. You will then see a public footpath sign on your left that will lead you down to the river and back to Kingswear. You can extend the walk at this point by continuing on to the next woodlands, Long Woods, which are part of the Dart Valley Trail and also owned by the National Trust. A lovely walk in itself.
6. We will take the short route back at this point, so take the footpath on your left down to the road. Be careful here it can be busy in the summer.
7. Turn left and walk down to the ferry crossing (you could always cross and walk through Dartmouth, then come back across on the lower ferry to Kingswear!). Cross the railway line and follow the footpath along the side of the railway towards Kingswear. You may need your walkers to put your lead on for this bit.
8. As you approach Kingswear and some railway buildings you can cross the railway tracks through a gate. Cross the railway here and you will come onto a very quiet lane. Then follow this lane back up to the car.

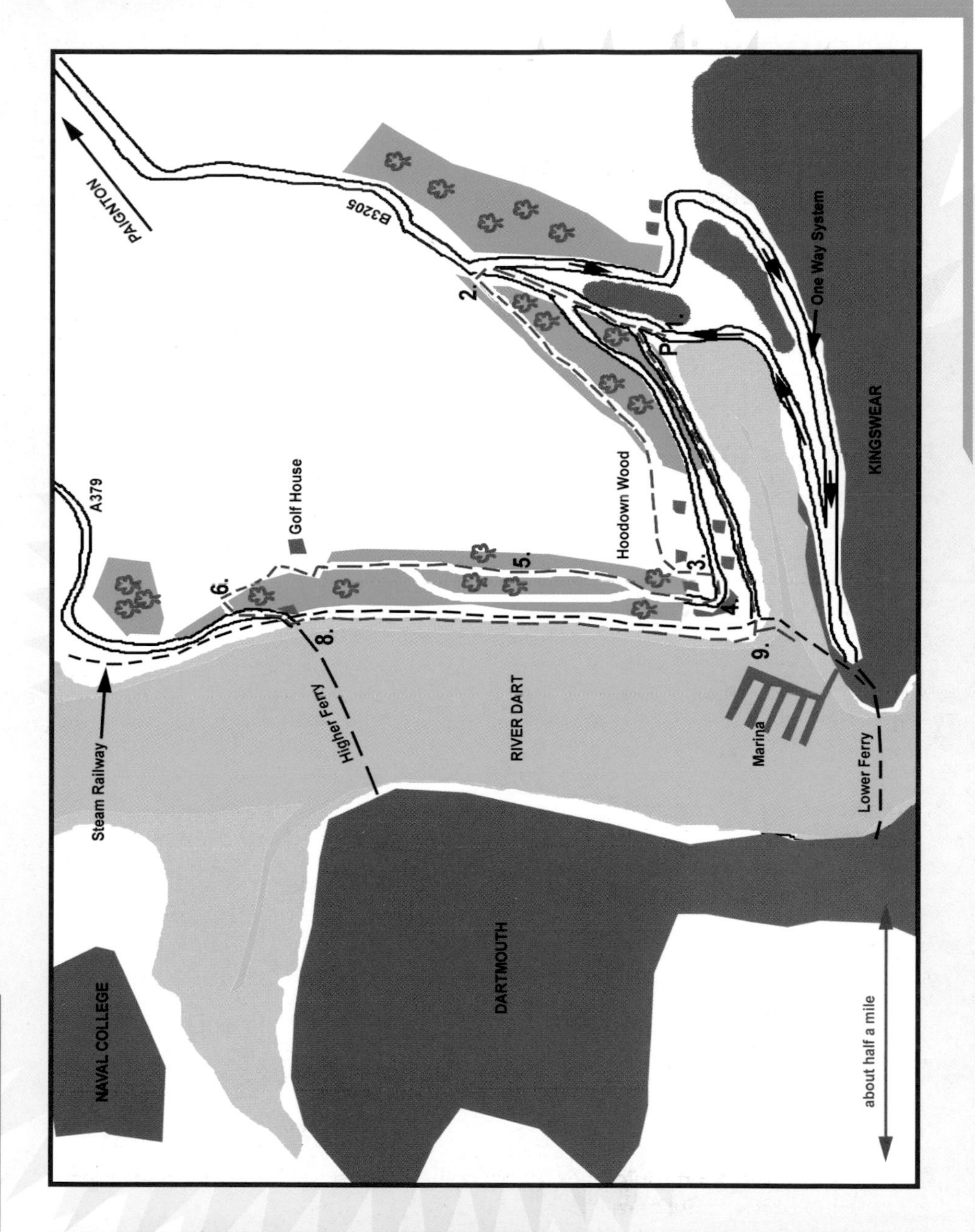

Playmates?	Y	Water to play in?	Y	Running space?	Y
Are there any hills?	Y	Any tricky stiles?	N	Car Parking?	Y
Are farm animals likely?	N	Poo Bins?	Y	Plenty of sticks?	Y

Walk 10 - Hembury Woods

Grid Reference: 730 680—Landranger 202   Distance: 2.5 miles (1.5 hours)

More lovely woods, with really well maintained paths, and probably the most beautiful stretch of the River Dart. I love jumping in the water here and having a good old swim. Then up to the fort to look at the views.

1. Turn off the A38 at Buckfastleigh and follow signs to the Abbey. Drive past the abbey entrance and left up to the top of the hill. At the crossroads at the top of the hill turn right towards Holne. Then immediately take the turning on your right. Follow this until you come to a left turn, go straight on following sign for Hembury Woods.
2. You go to the bottom of a hill and then drive into the woods and up the hill. Halfway up on your left you will see a parking area, ask your walkers to stop their car here.
3. Cross over and enter the woods by the path that is slightly downhill form the car park.
4. You will be in a walled path that leads down towards the river. Follow this down, being careful not to slip on the rocky surface.
5. At a junction follow sign right, downhill towards the river.
6. At the river stop and simply enjoy yourself before taking the steps up and around a damaged section of the river bank (this is quite a steep climb and descent!) Once you are back to the rivers edge, follow the path as far as it goes along the river bank, you will notice a gated cave entrance on your left at one point (little dogs should be careful not to go exploring in here!), a weir on your right and often quite a few walkers in boats playing around. I like to bark at them.
7. You will finally reach a sign on a gate that tells you that you are at the end of National Trust land. You now have to pull your walker up the hill. Take the left hand path that wiggles up a gravely track.
8. At the T-junction turn left along a level track.
9. You will soon come to a path that goes uphill on your right. If your walker is getting tired you can go straight on back to the car park. If they need more exercise, turn right up the hill. The trees look amazing up here!

10 and 11. You will reach a gate at the top. Go straight through onto the common, and follow the path around to the left and through another gate with large floppy paddles next to it. Maybe the walkers use these for some sort of game?

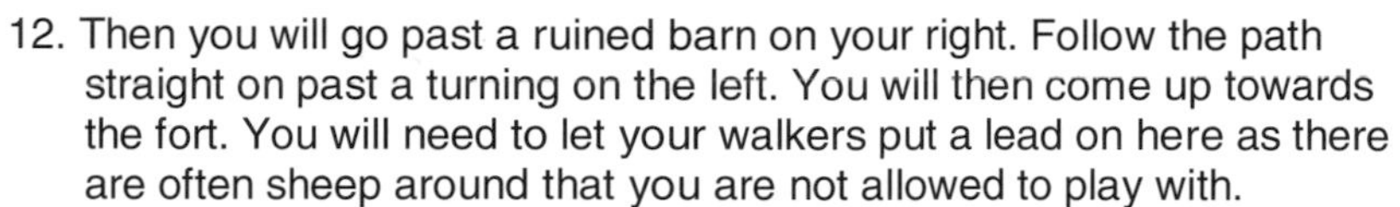

12. Then you will go past a ruined barn on your right. Follow the path straight on past a turning on the left. You will then come up towards the fort. You will need to let your walkers put a lead on here as there are often sheep around that you are not allowed to play with.
13. Once you have enjoyed the view, you continue across the common and down into the woods the other side, following a very wiggly path down through the woods back to the car park.

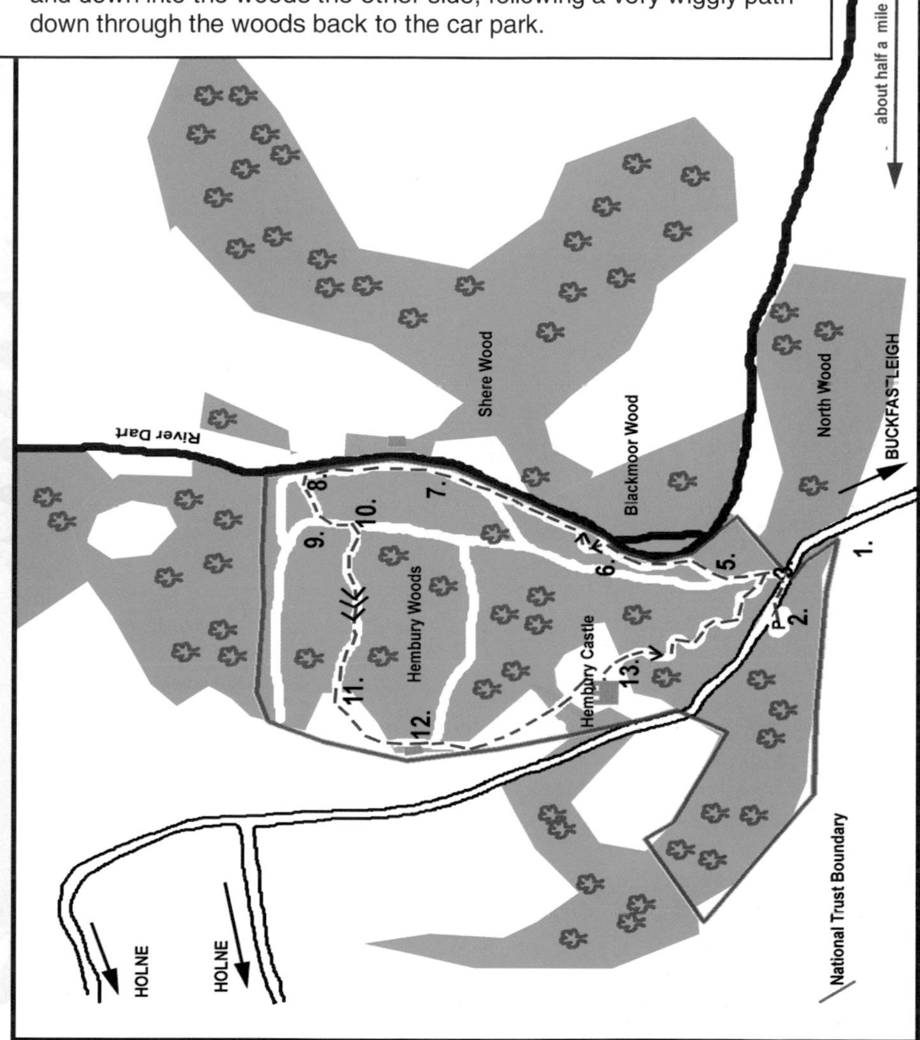

Playmates?	Y	Water to play in?	Y	Running space?	Y
Are there any hills?	Y	Any tricky stiles?	N	Car Parking?	Y
Are farm animals likely?	N	Poo Bins?	N	Plenty of sticks?	Y

Walk 11— Hardwick Woods

Grid Reference: 526 556—Landranger 201 Distance: 1 mile (45 mins)

Although this is not a very long walk, the views are lovely, the woods are very pretty and it is very convenient if you live in Plymouth.

1. Head into Plympton from the A38. Then take the first turn on the right through the industrial estate and across the railway bridge. You end up coming into a housing estate, you need to turn right at the first T-Junction you come to. This road should take you up and around the back of the woods that you can see on the top of the hill. As you drive out of Plympton you will see the A38 on your right. On your left you will see an obvious area to pull in and park in front of main entrance to woods.
2. Head into the woods going straight up the gentle hill, ignore the large path that goes off to the left.
3. Ignore the next path on the left that runs along the top of the hill.
4. At the T junction near top of hill bare right.
5. Then you will walk for some way down into woods. You will see a memorial post dedicated to the Cann's. At this post take a sharp left, almost back on yourself.
6. At a Y junction take the right fork. Ignore the sharp right that heads off down the hill towards Plympton.
7. There is a nice open field on the right which I like to go and have a run in if there are no farm animals about (also nice for a picnic).
8. At crossroads go straight ahead. Then follow path as it leads you back to the car. Ignore turns on right and left.

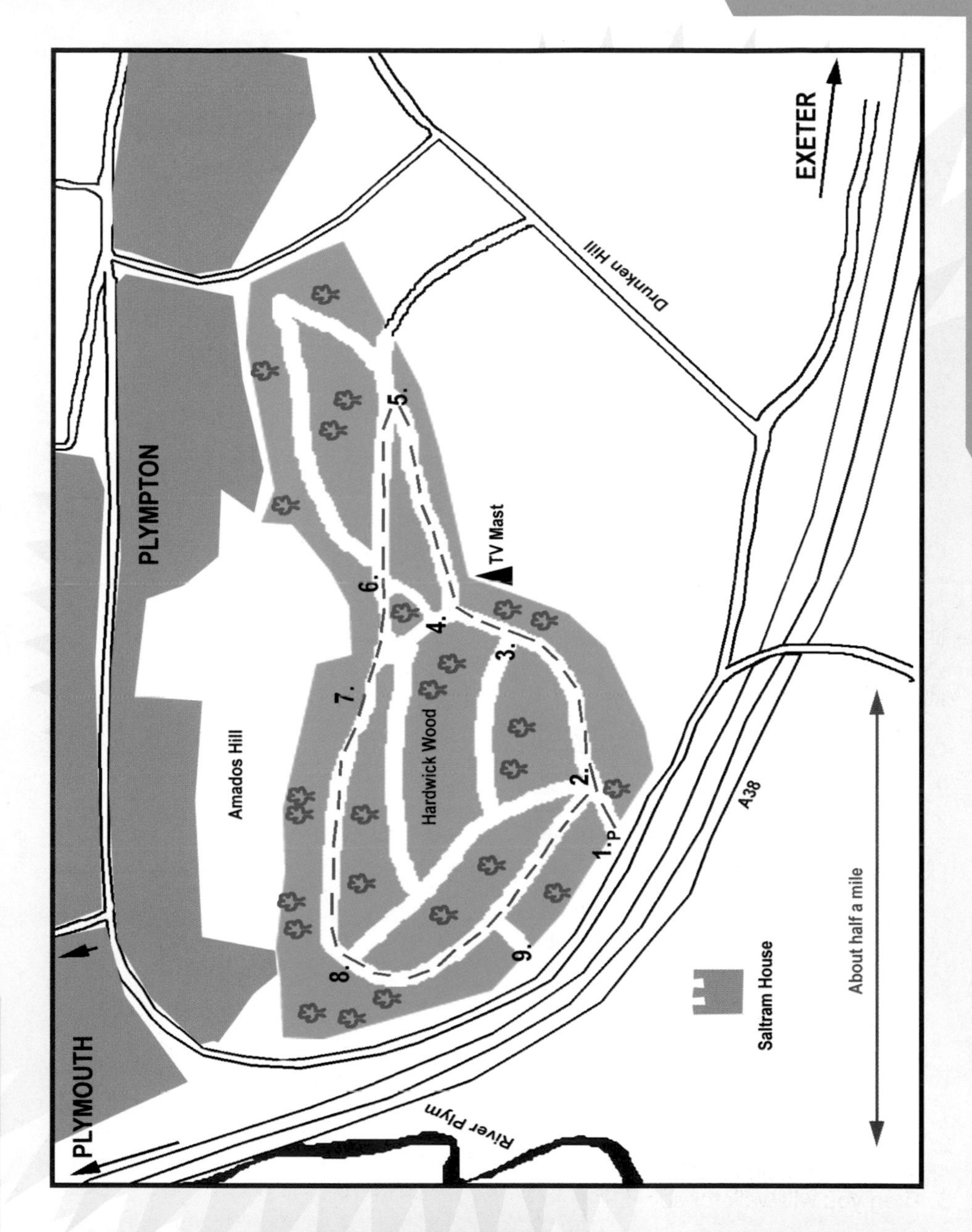

Playmates?	Y	Water to play in?	N	Running space?	Y
Are there any hills?	N	Any tricky stiles?	N	Car Parking?	Y
Are farm animals likely?	N	Poo Bins?	N	Plenty of sticks?	N

Walk 12— Loddiswell Railway

Grid Reference: 732484—Landranger 202	Distance: 2.5 miles (1.5 hours)

This is a great walk along an old railway embankment in South Devon. The walk is lovely and level with lots of water and woodland. I love it, and my walker really likes the old train station at the start of the walk

1. Your walker needs to take the A381 from Totnes or the A379 from Plymouth and head for Sorley Tunnel near Churchstow. Turn off and take the B3196 to Loddiswell. As you come to a bridge over the Avon at the bottom of the valley, turn right before the bridge and follow the road until you go under an old railway bridge . You will then see the old railway station on your left. Your walker needs to find somewhere to park without blocking the owner's gateways.
2. Ask your walker to put you on your lead for the first part of the walk (about 200 metres) down a narrow path next to the old station. Once past the end of this path you can come off your lead.
3. Then follow the river along until you reach another old railway bridge. Don't cross the bridge stay following the path along the riverbank you are already on. I like to hang around the old bridge for a while and play in the river.
4. You will wind your way up the valley until you find another railway bridge. This time you can cross the bridge and head back towards the car down the old railway track. My walker tells me that up until 40 years ago trains used to stop at Loddiswell. I think it is much nicer as a dog walk!

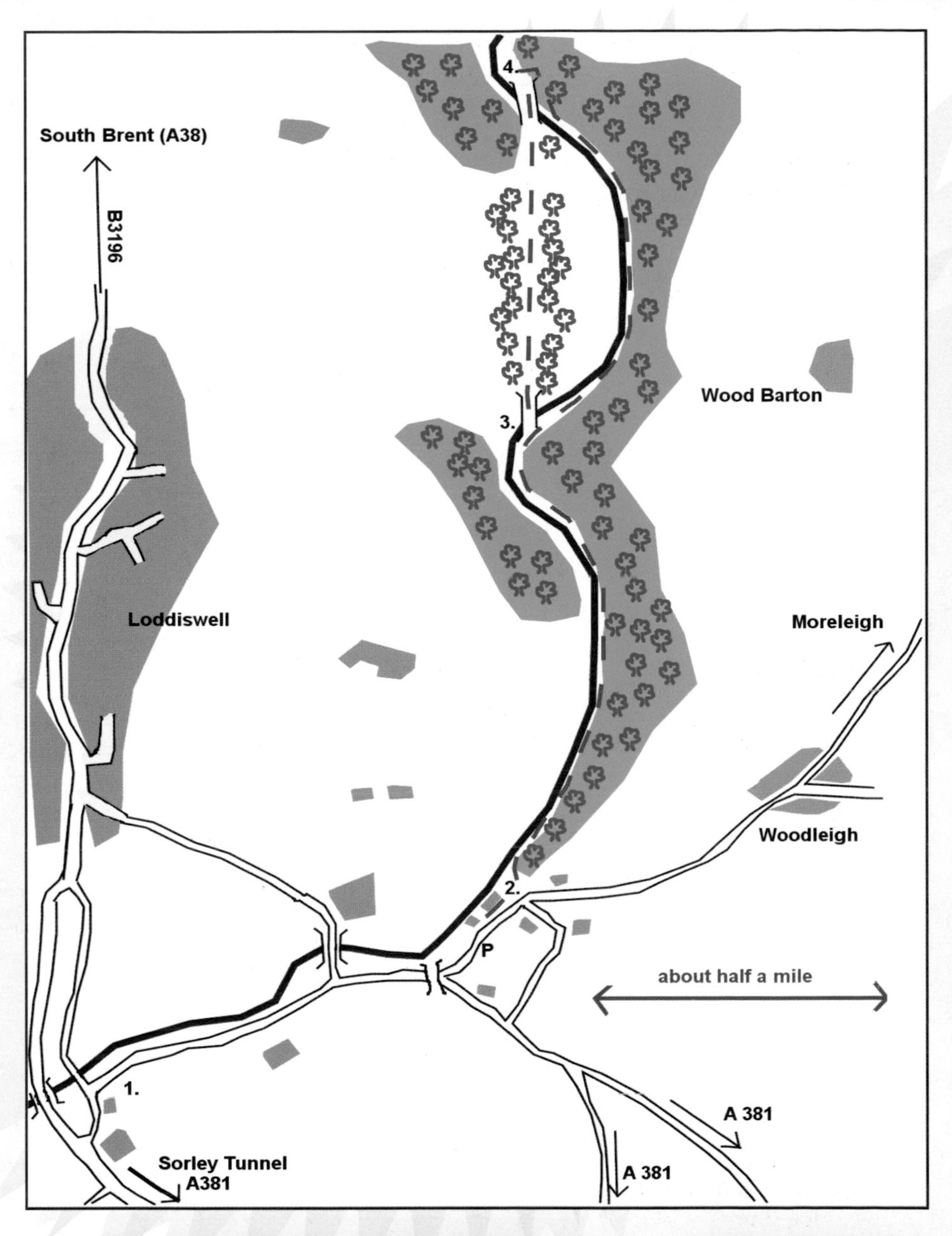

Playmates?	Y	Water to play in?	Y	Running space?	Y
Are there any hills?	N	Any tricky stiles?	1	Car Parking?	Y
Are farm animals likely?	N	Poo Bins?	Y	Plenty of sticks?	Y

Walk 13 - Aveton Gifford Tide Trail

Grid Reference: 692 473—Landranger 202   Distance: 2.5 miles (2 hours)

This is a lovely walk outside Aveton Gifford on the River Avon. You must check the tide time before doing this walk as you will not be able to get along the tide road at high tide. Anything above 3 metres will start to flood the road.

1. Take the A379 from Plymouth or the A381 from Totnes to Aveton Gifford (Nr Bantham) Park in the car park on the outskirts of Aveton Gifford. It is just next to the bridge over the River Avon. Park up and start walking.
2. Head off down the tidal road down the river. Lots of lovely mud to play in. You will get to the first creek on your right. Follow the footpath sign up the right of creek and across a set of stepping stones.
3. Follow footpath up onto a small lane. When you get to the lane turn right and follow it to a little hamlet.
4. Ignore a style and small lane to your left. Turn left up a steep hill once you have passed some small white cottages.
5. At the top of the hill turn left along a small lane that runs across the hill. This is called Drunkard's Lane! Some nice country views across to moors at the top.
6. Then the lane gets narrower and drops down to meet the main lane again. Go down the hill until you reach a small bridge.

7. You can choose here whether to turn left before or after the bridge as there are two footpaths back to the tidal road. If water is getting higher I would choose the one after the bridge.
8. At tidal road turn left back to car park.

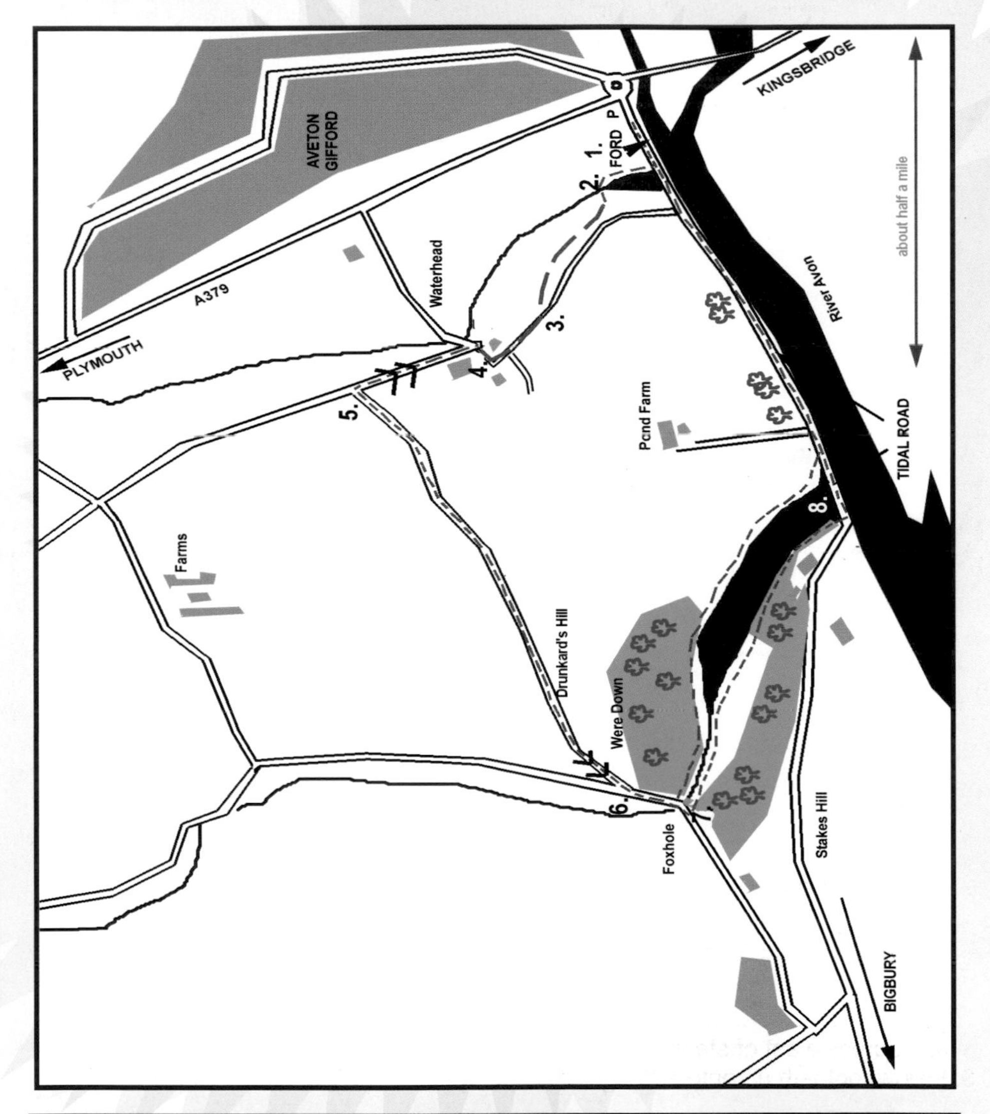

Playmates?	Y	Water to play in?	Y	Running space?	Y
Are there any hills?	Y	Any tricky stiles?	N	Car Parking?	Y
Are farm animals likely?	N	Poo Bins?	N	Plenty of sticks?	Y

Walk 14—River Plym Viaduct

Grid Reference: 524 585—Landranger 201 Distance: 2.5 miles (2 hours)

This is an incredible walk. My walker was amazed how wild the woods felt, although they are so near to Plymouth. The river Plym is stunning with amazing slate lining the bottom. The walk has loads of interesting things for your walkers to look at and lots of water and sticks for us dogs to enjoy. There are actually two main walks here. One gentle and one a little more challenging (for the walkers anyway).

1. Turn off the A38 at the main roundabout outside Plymouth and head towards Plympton. Take the first road on your right that you see signposted to Plym Bridge Woods Trail. Follow this road up out of Plympton, it eventually turns into a winding country lane that brings you to the car park near a disused railway bridge.
2. Get out and head onto the path that starts next to the railway bridge. Stay on this side of the river and start heading upstream on the path that runs along below the cycle trail. I like chasing bikes but my walkers don't find it very funny, so the separate path is great.
3. Follow the path up the river to the Viaduct (big bridge that used to carry trains, whatever they are?) Your walkers may want to check out the ruined quarry workings and read all the information boards. I prefer to stand on the bridge and gaze into the quarry hoping to see a Peregrine falcon, which breed here.
4. This is where you need to make a decision. If your walkers look tired then simply head back down on the other side of the river back to the car park. They could always throw a stick for you in the river meadows back at the start.
5. If they look fresh and 'waggy tailed' then you turn right just after the viaduct and take a track down to the river bank and carry on along the river past a weir and on.
6. You will eventually reach a grassy bit where the track turns up the hill away from the river. Follow this until you reach the cycle route again. Then turn left back to the viaduct.
7. When you reach the viaduct turn left before you cross and walk back down the river on the opposite side to the one you came up. Follow this path until you reach a road. Get your walker to put you on your lead for the short walk to the bridge that takes you back over the river to the car park.

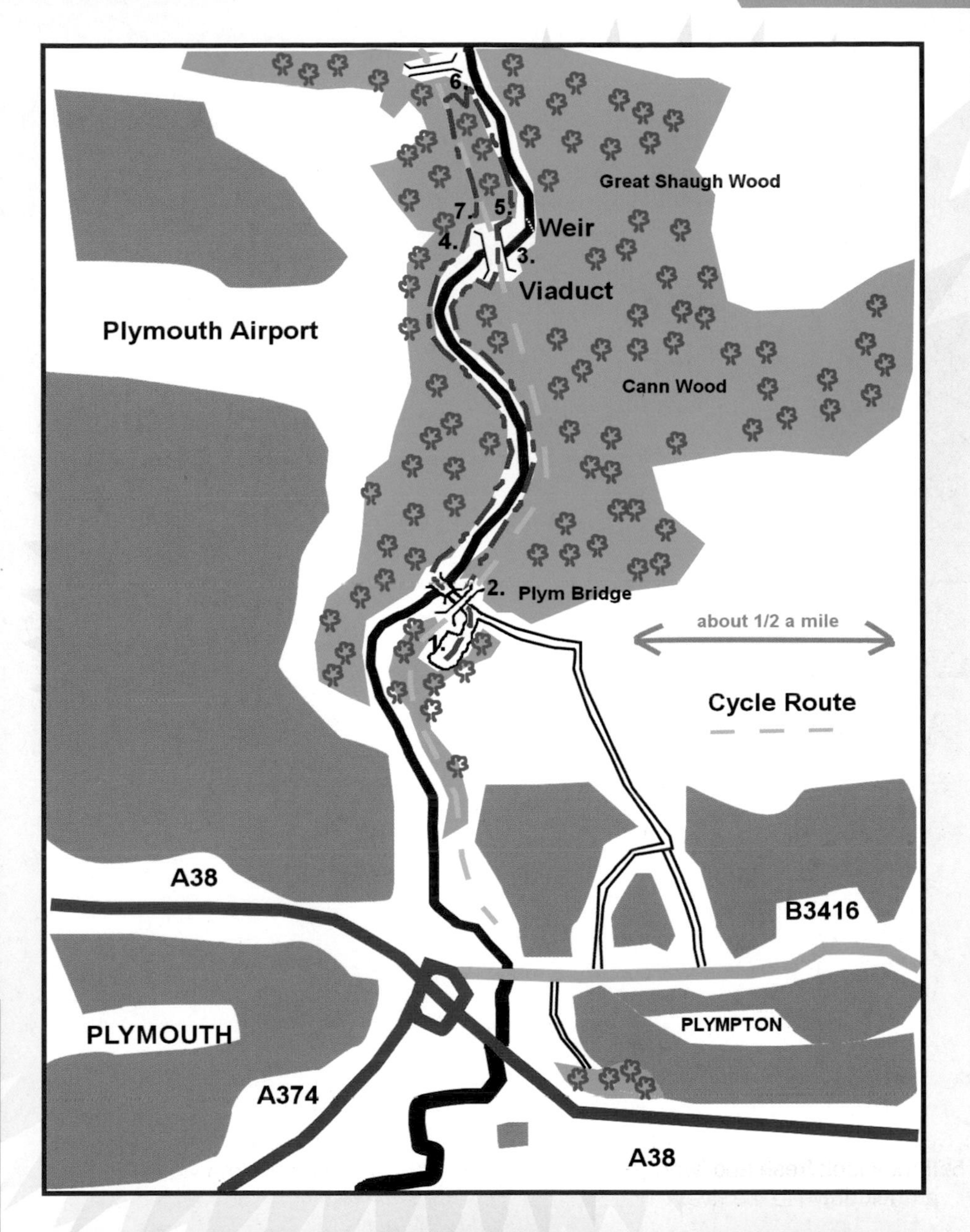

Playmates?	Y	Water to play in?	Y	Running space?	Y
Are there any hills?	Y	Any tricky stiles?	N	Car Parking?	Y
Are farm animals likely?	N	Poo Bins?	Y	Plenty of sticks?	Y

Walk 15—Ashclyst Forest

Grid Reference: 995 002—Landranger 192 Distance: 1 mile (45mins)

A beautiful walk with glimpses of Killerton House in the distance, magnificent trees and loads of lovely places for your walkers to sit and rest.

1. Get your walker to take the B3181 from Exeter towards Cullompton. Just after you pass the turning to Killerton House on your left you need to take a small lane on your right signposted to Caddihoe and Ashclyst Forest. Follow the lane passing some lovely estate cottages. Then pull into a parking area called Deadlands.
2. Lock up and head up the obvious track in front of you.
3. This walk is simple because you just have to follow the green path markers that are dotted along the way. At one point you can go straight on or turn right and go the opposite way around the loop. We always go straight on up to a big open area with benches in it.
4. The woods are varied and beautiful with some magnificent fir trees dotted around. I love to bark at the big trees in one of the open areas.

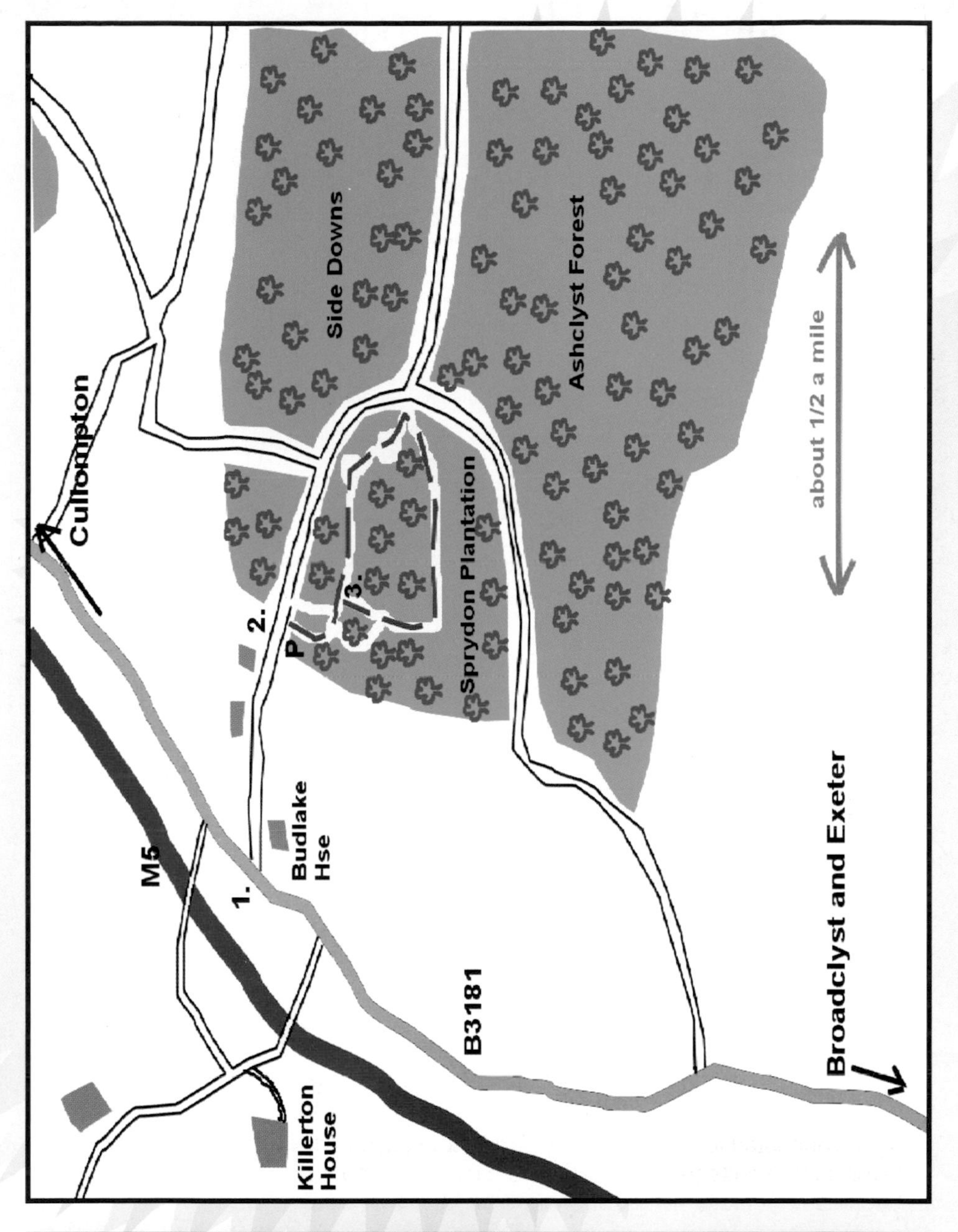

Playmates?	Y	Water to play in?	N	Running space?	Y
Are there any hills?	N	Any tricky stiles?	Y	Car Parking?	N
Are farm animals likely?	N	Poo Bins?	N	Plenty of sticks?	Y

Walk 16—Harpford Common

Grid Reference: 116 924—Landranger 192 Distance: 2 miles (1 hour)

This has to be one of my favourite walks. I am off the lead all the time and the views on the walk are probably some of the best in Devon. In fact on a good day it seems as though you can see most of Devon.

1. From the A30 take the A375 to Sidmouth and turn right at the Hare and Hounds pub on Putts Corner. Then turn left signposted East Hill strips and drive to the end of the ridge where there is an obvious car park. From Sidmouth take A375 and then take first left to Wiggaton, turn left into car park when you reach top of hill.
2. Once your walkers have parked you need to head away from the road down a large track that passes two 'no vehicle' signs. This is part of the East Devon Way.
3. Follow this track ignoring any tracks leading off down hills, until you reach an obvious fork in the track. Take the right hand fork (following Easy Devon Way).
4. You eventually come out on Harpford Common. Carry straight on until you get to the second public footpath sign pointing left, (there is a large fir tree and a telegraph pole at this junction.
5. Take a left here and walk along the ridge taking time to admire the view over most of East Devon. You can see Sidmouth below and all the way past Berry Head to your right, and over past Haytor and Saddle Tor inland. There is a nice bench for your walkers to sit on.
6. The path forks ahead, take the wider track that is above the other one.
7. Follow path into woods until you reach another large gravel track. Turn left and follow this back to the car park.

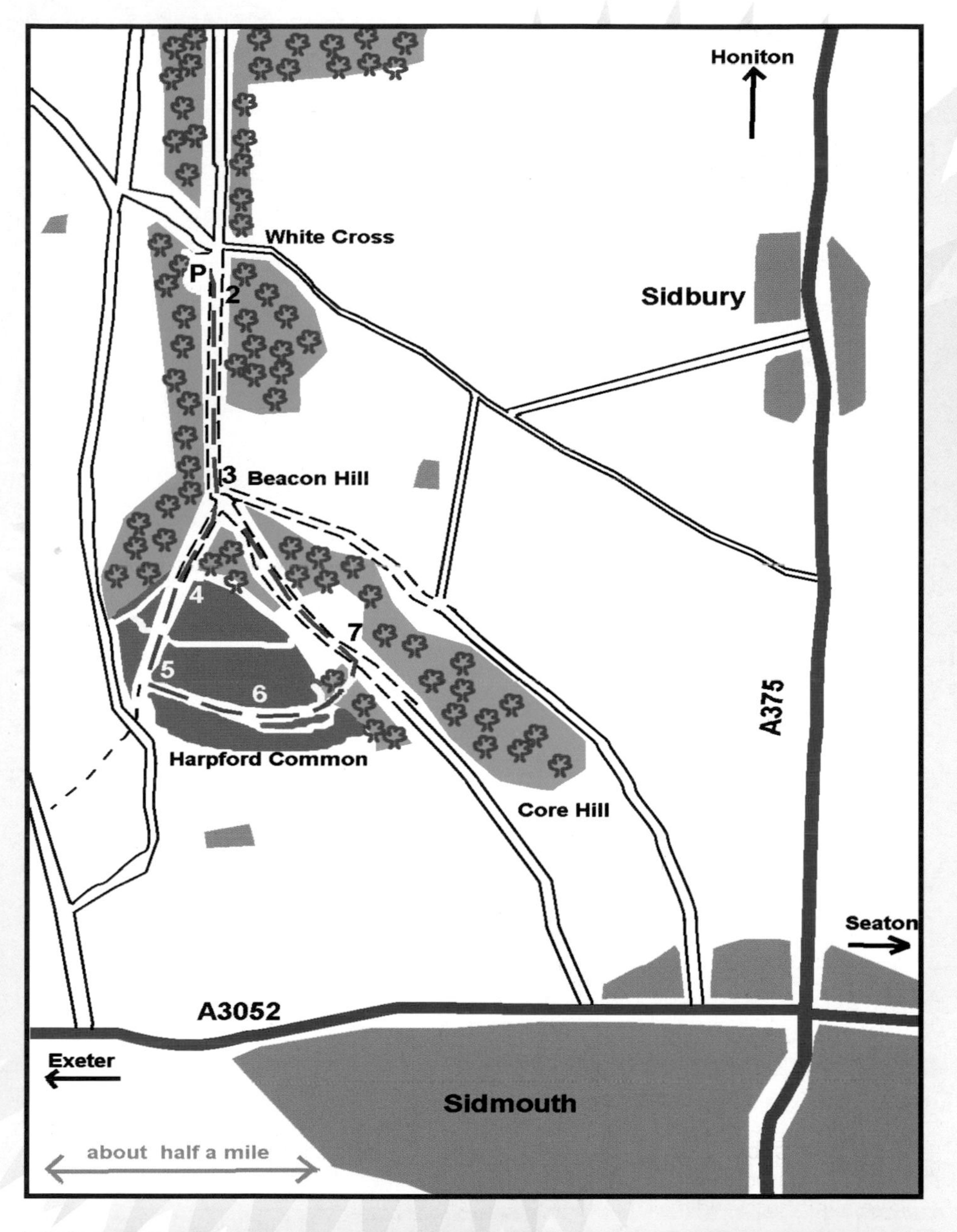

Playmates?	Y	Water to play in?	N	Running space?	Y
Are there any hills?	Y	Any tricky stiles?	N	Car Parking?	Y
Are farm animals likely?	N	Poo Bins?	N	Plenty of sticks?	Y

Toby's Directory

Run for Pet owners, by Pet owners.

- **Personal Service/Individual Cremations**
- **Collection and delivery service**
- **Open door practice/ Domestic Pets Only**
- **Offer a final farewell in our St.Francis Room**

3 Gidley's Meadow, Christow,Exeter, EX6 7QB

Tel: 01647 253053

www.valleypetcrematorium.co.uk

Sarah Louise Way
Dog & Cat Grooming

Tel:(01364) 652040
Or (01364) 631198

Dog walking service—Collection and return
Home visits to care for your pets
Dog boarding / Day creche in our home
Errands / House checks / Plant care

Contact Lorraine on:
Tel : 01752 563212
Mob: 07971 108012

National Petsitters
www.dogslt.com

Kistor Canine Beauticians

363 Torquay Road, Preston,
Paignton, TQ3 2BT

01803 521 597

Winners of National and International Awards in the art of dog grooming.

Toby's Directory

Toby's Directory

PET'S BEST FRIENDS

ANIMAL CARE IN YOUR OWN HOME

Dot & Jill

01626 872211 07877 565403

d.simmons@virgin.net jillconnole@hotmail.com

Canine authors

Are you and your walker interested in writing a Toby's Guide for your area?

We need you to find, and write, 14 high quality walks that are dog friendly.

Contact Alan to find out more

alan@scrivenhousebooks.co.uk

Dewerstone Photography

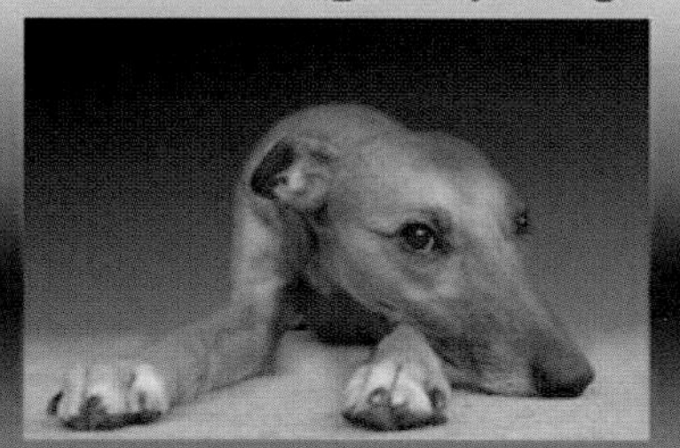

Canine Portrait Specialist

LOUISE TOPE

www.dewerstonephotography.co.uk

Plymouth, Devon. 01752 402086